The
HOWL.
Within

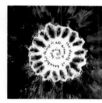

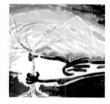

Jessica Aidley

ISBN: 978-1-910719-75-6

Published for Jessica Aidley by
Verité CM Limited,
124 Sea Place, Worthing, West Sussex BN12 4BG
+44 (0) 1903 241975
email: enquiries@veritecm.com
www.veritecm.com

British Library Cataloguing in Publication Data

A catalogue record for this book is available from the British Library

Printed in England

DEDICATION

I dedicate this book

to the memory of David,

and I dedicate it also to the living,

our children

Tim, Richi, Katie and Jack,

and

my new husband, John,

with all of whom I share love,

life and laughter.

FOREWORD

I wrote these poems as a way of coping with my grief after the death of my husband, and so they tell it as it was. They follow my journey from initial shock, desperate grief, through to learning to live without David, and then on to finding that there is love, life, and laughter in the 'after'.

David and I had been married for nearly 30 years, and had much enjoyed bringing up our four children, the last of whom had recently left home. His mother, Mollie, lived with us.

Then, 4 weeks before I was to be ordained priest, I found David dead in the garden.

In the same way that you keep on running for some steps after stubbing your toe badly, so I kept on following the plans that had been made for me to be ordained.

The poems in this book do not include those where I wrestled with my faith and with God, as I have decided to publish those separately; but the ones that are in this book were all written in the context of losing David so suddenly and unexpectedly just before I was ordained, and trying to make sense of his death in that context.

All but one of the images were also produced in response to grief, and as part of dealing with it, and they are therefore not meant to be perfect illustrations.

When I was grieving, I found other peoples' poems helped me to deal with my own grief, for it's a new world, and a new stage of life: it helped me to know I was not alone. I have published the poems in the hope that they will help you if you are grieving, or if you are trying to support someone else in their grief.

If you would like to contact me, my email is thehowlwithin@gmail.com

CONTENTS

9. OUT OF THE VALLEY

10. MOVING ON

11. GIVING THANKS

EPILOGUE

FRONTISPIECE

I started on a journey
through the valley
of the shadow of death
which I had no desire
to take,
but which I know,
from my own experience,
the Lord takes with us.

Often,
He has seemed very distant,
and often
I could not pray to him,
worship him,
or even feel his presence
but only felt
great rage against Him
but now I know,
that He was with me.

Sometimes,
always in the darkest places,
I would find Him.
It is in the darkest places
that the light shines brightest,
and in the dark valley
of the shadow of death
I have found the jewels of God:
His treasures of darkness.

I have also found
that the love
of those around me
who held me
in their prayers,
in some way,
cradled me.

I also know,
because
He has done this for me,
that the Lord
does guide our feet
back into the ways of peace,
and that joy,
and laughter,
do enter our lives again,
and that God, our God,
is a God of compassion,
who walks with us.

INTO THE VALLEY

In My Head

In my head
I still hear
the cry
that each
of my family
uttered
when I told them
the news.

How I wish
the ears
of my memory
were
deaf.

That Day That You Died

That day that you died,
the sun shone so beautifully,
with its promise of endless days,
of pleasures still to come.
Deceitful sun.

That day that you died,
was a sleepy afternoon,
with drowsy bumblebees
harvesting the flowers,
and endless time.
Time ended now.

That day that you died,
was full of laughter,
the laughter of life and love
reflecting the glory of the day.
Dangerous day.

The day that you died
the lawn was freshly mown by
you,
smooth and ordered to receive
you
as you lay down to die,
Treacherous grass.

That day that you died,
The light of the sun was upon
the grass,
but the shadow of your body
darkened the ground;
harbinger of the
darkness that has come.

That day that you died,
the hand of God was upon us
to put asunder that which he
had made.
The two, who had been one,
cloven into two again,
leaving me
to face the mocking sunlight
alone...

That day that you died,
what became of you?
When I was left here
where did you go?

Telling His Mother

On a golden sunlit afternoon
he had been living
now he was dead.

And I,
I
had to tell
his mother,
she being
just the
first
of many.

She sat,
frail curled and old,
in her usual
chair,
with fragile heart
and fragile
mind,
but safe
and comfortable
… for now.

How to tell her?
With hammer-cracking
panic
distorting my thinking?
How could I tell her
such a thing?

I started to skirt
round the edge
of our known world,
to the truth
beyond,
my pussy-footing
skating sharply
on the thin ice
of her equanimity.

"Something terrible
has happened"
I said.

"What's that dear?"

"It's David"

"David?"

"He's collapsed."

"He's in the garden."

"He was mowing."

"He's had a heart attack."

"I'm sorry,"

"but – "

"he's died."

"He will get better, though,
– won't he?"

"No.
He's had a heart attack
and he's died."

"He will get better
– won't he?"

"No."

Silence,
like frozen water,
hanging
in the air.

Then crack
thunder-cracking
two heads,
two lives,
quarry
blasted.

Walking in the Valley

I'm walking in the valley,
in the valley of the shadow of death.
The death was not my own,
but of him whom I loved,
the one who was half of me.

It's dark in here,
dark and troubled.
The coldness is deep, so deep.
and there's no way back
into the sunshine,
no way at all.

I can see,
only shadows of lost things,
lost love, lost hope.
The uneven ground
causes me to stumble
and I, too, am lost...

for I'm walking

walking in the valley

walking in the valley

of the shadow of death.

The Cleaver of God

The cleaver
of God
hung over us
from the first day
that we were
made one
in marriage.

We did not know it,
nor sense it,
until the day
it struck
out of the blue
shattering the sunlight
to drive us apart.

So now I
fear
the cleaver
of God
for who
will he strike
next?

The Burying

As tall as my love stood above the earth
so lies he deep beneath it,
drawn into the clay that gave him birth.
the essence and being of him
lost;

Lost. Only the frame, the image of him,
is there
slowly changing,
until there will remain only bones where
now his cold and lifeless body rearranging
lies.

Lies, lies they tell that say that he is here,
here with me and them,
they say they sense his presence in the air
but he's gone, gone from them and
me.

Me. Once his wide open arms welcomed me
with such tenderness and care,
he would sing and tell me of his love
his precious face holding mine in a
smile.

Smile. That smile had gone when I found him
lying heavily on the ground,
his life had fled, leaving only the crying
the burying ... the losing ...
of the dead.

Lie Gently Under the Earth

Lie gently under the earth,
my dearest love,
coffin-cradled in the soil
the promise of new birth.

Be at peace, at one again
with that from whence you came
and let no part trouble you
of the echoes of my pain.

Lie gently under the soil, dear one
enfolded in God's care
leave me now, and worship him
through his beloved Son.

May your precious soul be free
to soar on eagle's wings
not crippled, scarred or spoilt
by being torn from me.

In a poem I once read
that love is in the letting go
but oh my love, I cannot now
admit to me that you are dead.

TWO

A DIFFERENT LANDSCAPE

No Amount of Longing

No amount of longing,
no amount of pain
will make my beloved
come back to me again.

Today, as Weeping

Today, as weeping,
I drove home
from shopping,
as I have
so often done
since he died,
I thought to myself;
can they prosecute you
for driving
whilst under
the influence of emotion?

I See the world

I see the world through
the losing of you;
I see it in that way.

The world may see me smile,
and answer rationally,
but inside my mind
I'm thinking of you.

I may be speaking lightly
of interesting things,
but everything I say
is tinged with you.

I may be singing hymns,
apparently devout,
but the lines and the words
remind me of you.

I may be making plans,
but they are not real,
I'm just pretending,
because I live in the past
where you lived with me.

It is in the Moving

"I can see him still –
sitting there."
they say.

It's odd,
for when I see him
(in the eye of my mind)
he is always moving.

Coming round
the corner of the house,
walking through the door,
washing up,
or striding from St Peter's.

Only when I concentrate
can I see him
sitting still
– at rest –
in his green leather chair.

But for me
it is in the moving
that the memory
takes me by surprise

This Spring

This Spring the hazel twigs
are showing green
against the dead branches of winter.
The snowdrops are displaying their innocence
amongst the pressed grass
of the once snow-laden lawn;
but my love has no life in him,
he will not see these signs of life,
or feel his heart lift
with the joy of Spring.

This Spring the daffodils, which he loved so much,
have pushed their spears
through the sodden earth and weary grass,
to lift towards the sky
their loaded heads of gold.
But my love will not lift his head,
nor show his beloved face to the sky,
his breath will not mingle with the breezes
which March has brought
between the showers.

This Spring the haunting cry of owls
once again fills the deepness of the night,
one calling to his love
and the other answering,
but in this darkness,
you cannot call to me my love,
nor can I answer you,
there is no Spring for us.

This Spring, in which a flaunting God
shows yet again the wonders of his mind,
will not belong to those who lie
beneath the sodden earth,
but only serve to emphasise
in cruel parody,
all that we have lost.

No, there is no Spring for us.

My Father Died

My father died,
and my mother said,
'How can I be alive
when he is dead?'

I heard what she said
with my ears,
I thought I knew
what she meant,
but I did not understand.

I heard what she said
with my mind
I thought I knew
how she felt,
but I did not understand.

I heard what she said
with my spirit
and my heart
went out to her
but I did not understand.

Now my husband has died
and I have said,
'How can I be alive
when he is dead?'

And I hear what she said
with my mind
and I hear what she said
with my spirit:

Now,

too   late   to   help,

I understand.

The Lie of His Belt

The lie of his belt
around his hips,
the colour of his trousers.

Zigzag patterns across the chest
of the 'old man' cardigan.

The gentle stoop,
and the saggy jacket.

The folded face
and the smiling eyes.

The way of walking
with the leather shoes.

All these things
when glimpsed
out of the corner of my eye
have the power
to lurch my heart

'it is him!'
'it is him!'

'is it him?'

oh please

let it be him?

I Just Want to be Held

Two years is a long time
without being touched,
really touched,
and held.

The dogs are warm
so cuffly to feel and hold,
but they don't hold me
in loving arms
as you once held me.

It's good to be hugged
by friends,
and held
(as some of them do)
for long enough
for the hug to soak in
and be absorbed.

But the daily touch,
the loving hug,
the embrace that is part
of passing in the kitchen
or the hall,
or lying in bed at night,
that is what I hunger for,
that is what I miss.

Touch

I used to be held,
enfolded and hugged,
because he loved me,
and I,
with all that I am,
loved him.

I used to be touched,
on the arm,
on the breast,
down my back,
because his love
was expressed
with his hands.

And we used to lie together,
behind and before,
warm and friendly,
curling to sleep,
one flesh,
together.

Now? Now it's different,
There's a sort
of empty space
on my skin,
a place of touching
no longer touched,
and hunger,
for those arms about
my shoulders.

I suppose,
in my widowhood,
I must learn
to go without.
I must close down
that within me
which needs that
touching
knowing that the
days of hugging
kissing
and sharing our love
are gone…

And for now,
now in this present
I inhabit,
I will remember
your touching,
and come to accept
in gratitude,
those hugs of love
which are like
those of our loving
felt
through a glass darkly.

Colour Me Black Today

Colour me black today,
let the material
that encloses my body
hold in itself
the warp and weft
of my being.

'Why don't you wear
something
just a bit more
colourful?'
they say,
'it might make you
feel a little better'.

Obediently,
I encase myself
in brighter cloth
but it isn't me;
it isn't me at all,
and I fling it aside
in despair.

I have a need
for my outer covering,
to share the darkness
which has invaded me,
and I find inside
an aversion
to being visible
in the remaining shadows
of my life.

THREE

CALLING TO HIM
ACROSS THE CHASM

Your Life Was Just a Fingerprint

You life was just a fingerprint
on the glass of eternity
soon to be washed off
and disappear.

Your Life Touched Mine

Your life touched mine.
First just in the being
noticed,
appreciated,
and
with the sharing
of minds.

Greater closeness came,
love with marriage,
the intertwining of our years
for a third of a century,
the growing of children
amongst our loving.

But then your time with me
was ended –
so abruptly ended –
on that day of sunlight
so darkly rotten
at its core.

The touch of your life
upon mine
was withdrawn,
recoiling suddenly
leaving me
limping
from the wound of loss.

What was the time
we had together?
a mere whisper
in the conversation of history,
a sigh upon the wind,
virtually nothing
in the aeons of eternity,
but everything
absolutely everything
to me

Walking to St Peter's

I remember you walking,
in the sunshine,
to St Peter's,
your jacket slung
over your shoulder,
your finger through the loop.

I remember you striding
along the lane,
bright tie showing
against your shirt,
upright and happy
on your way to church.

I remember you smiling
as I passed,
in the car,
smiling and waving
as I went ahead,
with all the heavy things.

I remember you, my love,
and it hurts
to remember,
as I drive along
that empty road,
and you're not there.

Sundays

Sitting in Church,
with you not there beside me,
an agonising empty space.
No hand to touch,
or shoulder to lean against,
no sense
of your presence,
nothing.

The sound of your voice
deep and moving,
the sight of your tears
as God's spirit flowed,
part of my worship
at one with you
in Him.

I ache to hear your voice,
to hear you singing,
to hear you praying.
I feel so much your loss
as I kneel before my Lord
to receive the bread
and the wine.

Then the walking home,
the unbearable absence,
you no longer beside me
holding hands
as we scoot the pebbles
down the road
in friendly play.

Anticipation of Sunday lunch
and shared afternoons
with Sunday papers
gently dozing,
the time to be
with each other,
now gone.

Sundays used to be golden days,
but now the very things
which made them good
serve only to emphasise
the loss,
the loneliness,
in the absence of you.

Today I Watched You

Today I watched you,
living and moving,
talking and smiling,
with the family.
I heard your voice,
watched you smile,
heard
and knew again
your tenderness.

But in all this,
you were not with me,
I could not reach out
and touch you.

You were but an image
on a video,
so tantalisingly there,
but here no more.

How I wish,
oh I wish so urgently,
that you were here,
with me.

When I look Into the future

When I look into the future and you're not there,
I am afraid:
When I think of living without you,
my spirit fails me.

My glance falls upon a photograph
of your precious face,
I think that I will not see you again,
and my heart spins.
I see something you have written,
just a note to the milkman,
I long to treasure it,
because you are no more.

I see the garden bathed in sunlight,
empty, because you are not in it.
I see the lawn green and fresh
with spring,
and growing,
purposeless,
without you.

I find the slides we took together,
now useless,
because we cannot share them.
The pictures in the album
now in my mind, alone.

I see the books you have written,
now to become outdated.
I hold the books you treasured
which I will never read,
what value have they now?

I see your ties, your hat upon the hook,
your toothbrush, and cricket on TV
I hear something funny
but I cannot tell you.

When I look into the future and you're not there,
I am afraid:

You Don't Need Me Anymore

You don't need me anymore,
for whether you are dead,
and finished,
and integral only
with the earth,
or whether you have entered
heaven's door,
and are filled now
with awe and wonder,
and steeped in glory,
you don't need me anymore

as I need you.

Colours of Loss

When first you died
the shards of my life
were like a
broken stained glass window
sharp kaleidoscope
piercing feelings
acute awareness
of things long unseen.

Alongside the tearing
of your roots from me
came visions of
acutely beautiful things
lit up by the lightning flashes
of my grief,
and I saw, as I had not seen,
since I was a child.

But now that transient
unsuspected glory is gone,
and the world is grey
and colourless
without you,
run through
by rivers of sadness
and sodden November
flooding.

Only old age is left,
no youth can come again
or dreams be fulfilled,
just the living out
of the death-sentence
of life
and its decay.

I had thought,
before,
of old-age as a gentle thing
trimmed with reminiscences;
a slow forgetting
and a gradual acquaintance
with the kindliness
of appropriate death.

But it's not like that,
it's the accumulation of
knowledge
of the horror of living
and the indignity
of dying,
of other's pain,
reflecting my own,
inevitable,
and universal,
and the realisation
that life is never good
for very long
or for very many.
How could God
have thought it was?

I Would That I

I would that I had made more use
of the time you had with me
That I had taken each day's cup
and drunk it to the full,
then taken it once more
and drained its every drop.

I would that I had really looked
at every fold and crease
that smiled about your face
impressing the very lines of them
upon my memory.

I would that I had gazed more often
into your loving eyes,
and answered then
with a generous heart
the questions that they asked.

I would that I had given you
more freely of my time,
and not put off to a later date
the lingering walks,
and explorations
that you so longed to make.

I would that I had lived each day
as if it was our last,
giving to you all of me
each minute of each hour –
not wasting the time we had.

If I had known the Lord would take
your life away so soon,

how
differently
I
should
have
lived.

40

I Awoke Today

I awoke today
determined to think
positive thoughts,
not to stray
into the place of pain
where memories of you
insistently
dwell.

I was determined,
and yet –
I failed.

God and Man Together

God and Man together
have laid their hands
upon this garden,
and now it shows
the glories of its Creator
and the works
of the hands of men.

How can I be alone
surrounded by this glory?
The waving tresses
of the willow trees,
the marbled shade
upon the secret lawns,
and the infinite sky
reflected in the water.

And yet it is said
that Adam in his paradise
walking and talking
freely with God
had need,
not of another man,
but of a woman
his other half.

So it is for me
in this special place
knowing that I have children
friends and family:
Knowing and loving God,
yet finding life
unending and unbearable
without you.

Doing the Christmas Cards

Doing the Christmas cards
is like walking along a path
with varied scenery,
all of which
reminds me
of you.

Looking down the avenues
into the past pleasures
of our friendships,
all of which
we enjoyed
as two.

Something's wrong in walking
down the trails of time
alone and without you
just me writing
to those
you knew.

But mostly it's a highway,
a route of remembrances,
with pain-filled potholes
travelling from the
before
to the after.

Changing

I know that I am changing,
that I am no longer
the person I was
when you died.
I know,
most of the time,
that you are dead,
and that I must live
without you.

I know that life is changing,
that I must plan ahead
in your absence
and,
as what I am now,
single
widowed
and alone.

I know the aloneness
is also changing,
that I share it
with my family,
and my friends.

I know that ahead
There is a path
for me to walk in,
that He has made His way
the way of light
and life and joy
amongst the sorrow ..
BUT
and it is a big 'but'
I
STILL CANNOT BELIEVE
THAT YOU ARE GONE!

FOUR

THE HOWL WITHIN
(speaking the pain)

Oh Death

Oh death,
where is thy sting?
they ask, who do not know;
I'll tell you where it is,
it's in the heart of me,
thrashing and stinging,
where only love should be..

The howl within

Comes not from broken bones
Or broken bruised skin:

It comes from being torn in two

In the losing of you

46

The Howl Within

The howl within
comes not
from broken bones,
or bruiséd skin;
it comes from being
torn in two,
in the losing
of you.

Can You See My Scream?

Do you want to see my scream?
I'll open my mouth
so you can see it
if you look.

Just as a child
opens their mouth
and places the tip of their finger
to show you the place
and says,
'Do you want to see my wobbly tooth?'
so I wonder,
if you look down my throat,
is the scream there for you to see?

And, if I look down Your throat,
is there a scream down there
too?

It's the 'Never'

It's the 'never' I find so hard
to grasp
and hold in my mind and being.
I still have difficulty accepting
that you won't ever
be coming back.

The never being able to hold you again,
nor tell you things
that are important,
the never being able to share with you
moments of delight,
or of pain.

It's never being able to relax with you
in quiet and gentle
companionship,
nor work side by side with you
in the kitchen,
with no need to talk
just getting on together.

But, most of all,
it's not being able to share with you
the awfulness
of your loss,
and not having you to help me
through the worst days
of my life.

Grief is a Fickle Thing

Grief is a fickle thing
with rules of its own
pulling on the threads of time
through 'our' past,
and my 'now',
and such as is to come.

It hangs around the corners
of my mind,
and will not let it go,
urging it to look
at this and that,
those diamond points of loss
with their incisive hurts.

Like a tidal wave
over the seas of my mind
it passes,
stirring up the pains and angers
from the seabed
of my unconscious
in chaotic turmoils.

Then, unnoticed,
it slides away
into the primal soup
of my spirit,
leaving me safe and calm
to face the day,

But, just when I think
I'm rising above it,
and know it for what it is,
it returns,
doubly malevolent,
to overwhelm
and devastate again.

Oh yes,
grief is a fickle thing
with rules of its own.

Leviathan

I thought you'd gone
you creeping, lurking
Leviathan of the deep.
The waters of grief were calmer,
and the turbulence
quieter
and more reflective.

But deep beneath
your tentacles were still
exploring the
dangerous places
of the watery depths
of my being.

Then you rose,
churning the waters,
tightening your grip
on my heart
so that it ached,
clenched with the sense of loss,
gripping my throat
as wave after wave of
weeping
convulsed my being
as uncontrollable as labour pangs
but with nothing to birth
but red eyes
swollen lids
and a sense of despair.

Will you always be there
waiting,
waiting to catch me unawares
and drowning hope?

When I am Driven

When I am driven to the point
where pain and despair rise
in flailing limbs
and slapping hand
finding release only
in stinging skin
and liquid pain
what am I doing?

Where is the strength on which I draw?
Whose salve am I applying
to my brokenness?
On whom am I depending?

In my hitting and my hurting
am I using one weakness
to outwit and outweigh another?

Can I bear to meet head-on
the pain that I feel
in the stillness
in the void
where you
once were?

What do I do with the Pain?

A year ago my beloved died,
leaving me behind,
in the innermost parts
of me
he also left
the anger and the pain.

The loss of him consumes my
thoughts
my very being,
warping the sinews of my body,
and my mind
in a frenzy
as they both distort my soul.

There is pain at being torn
apart,
at being forced
to live this life without him
no help available
from him who went and died.

I am angry at being left
at such a time
when I would be needing him
so much
just for surviving
for getting through this life.

I cannot be angry at you, Lord
for you did not
choose that my love should die
that day;
but is, instead,
the one who will redeem his
death.

I cannot be angry at my love,
for he did not
choose to lie down and die
to leave me
all alone
to face the future without him.

There was no shadow side to
him
longing
to be taken from this life,
instead
his was planning
with courage, joy, and hope.

So as this anger and pain grips
my very being
how do I get it out of me?
how do I get rid of it?
Lord, I cry out to you
for help.

In the Midst of Grieving

Last Thursday,
in the midst of grieving,
came a gift,
it was a day of happiness
clear and free
of the burden of loss,
lit up with inner laughter
and praise of You.
A day for singing in the car
my love of You.
Lifting my heart up to You
in praise and worship.
A day for seeing the
world around me
fresh and new,
a day with a future
and that
with hope in it.

For that gift,
I thank You
and I praise You
Lord.

Watersmeet

Two rivers fall
through their valleys
meeting where
the heron stands,
waiting for the fish.

I climb along,
over dark wet
autumn-strewn boulders
to the pool
below the water fall.

And, as I stand
I see how the waterfall
is your dying,
and the still deep pool
the time when
life was held in unbelief
that you had died.

The water pouring
through the narrow exit
like the torrent of knowing
of your loss,
followed by the rushing
of water between the rocks;
the tumultuous white chaos
of grief for you.

Then standing
on the high rocks
above that pool
which called me
so deeply;
the picture in my mind
of jumping in,
pulling me to hurtle down
and join you
in my drowning.

My friend –
perceiving –
calls to me
and I take shelter
from the river
on her other side,
withdrawing from you,
and the tempting river,
back into
my right mind.

Even by the writing
of this poem
I protect myself
from ever jumping,
for only
'by accident'
could I ever do it,
and they would know
that it wasn't.

Mathematical Thought...

My love has died
leaving this pain
in my heart
and of those
who loved him.

If I should decide
to end this pain
and take my life
that pain
is multiplied
for all but me.

What gift
would I lay then
at my Lord's feet
but yet more broken lives
and absolute
defeat?

FIVE

WITHDRAWAL

The poems in this section were written in one of the darkest parts of my grieving, and may be hard to read.

Two Snails

Delicately banded
with gold and brown,
the snail glides in the sunlight
along the edge of the leaf,
The light reveals
a gentle gleam
upon the smooth surface
of its translucent shell.

Moving, it collides
in slow motion
with a light-filled
drop of dew;
The water moves
over its gliding
softness,
giving it life.

A gently waving tentacle
with caviar eye at tip
touches the future
and does not recoil,
only moving in and out
telescope-like
exploring space.

The other snail
is a beast of the night,
earth-brown shelled,
leaver of silvered trails
on the stony ground,
and silent mover
in the darkness.

It's a troglodytic
dweller in holes
and under stones.
It hides from the gardener
and the thrush,
the weather and the sun.

It's exploring tentacles
reaching tentatively forward
touch sharp painful things
and in a convulsion of fear
draw back
inside themselves.

As wave after wave of
searing hurts
assault its brown
and wrinkled body
it pulls its whole self
inside its shell
and seals the opening.

I used to be
like the first snail
in the sunlit days
of my loving,
but now
I am the second snail,
and I wish I could
totally withdraw
into my shell
and stay there.

I Want to...

I want to climb into a hole.
Just curl up in a ball
and die.

It isn't that
there are not things
worth living for:-
my children, family
and my friends;
It's the living – without him –
that never ends.

It's the daily renewal
of the learning
of his departure:
It's the knowing
that he'll never be here
with me
again.

It's the hoping
for his returning
from some far off distant
journey –
and the awful knowledge
that he'll never return,
that his journey
is no journey at all,
but a full stop.

It's the seeing of his picture
smiling out at me,
and knowing
that I'll never see
his face again,
and watch it as it moves
in loving laughter.

It's the longing
for his arms
around my shoulders
encircling me,
but knowing only
barren space
where they're supposed to be.

It's the lying in bed
curled up
without his warm presence
behind me,
the losing of
his friendly protection.

It's the pictures in my mind
of him
where he used to be,
walking head up to the sun,
and now...
so unbearably...
not there,
that's what
I can't stand.

So let me climb into a hole.
Just curl up in a ball
and die.

If I Walk

If I walk quietly, gently
can I occupy less space
and make no sound
to mark my passing
or to be marked by Him?
Can I enter a quiet oblivion
where love is not hounded by pain
nor joy stalked by grief?

Is there a place where
I can become as nothing?
I am tired of being
and of hurting
I am soul-weary of
days, weeks and months
of paying for my love of you.

Could I, like Alice, become
small enough
for the pain to be bearable
or even disappear
and for my feelings
to become as nothing?

Will there not come a time when
I have paid enough
for having loved you too much
and can come to a place
where I no longer
get dragged into the
mires of dangerous grief?

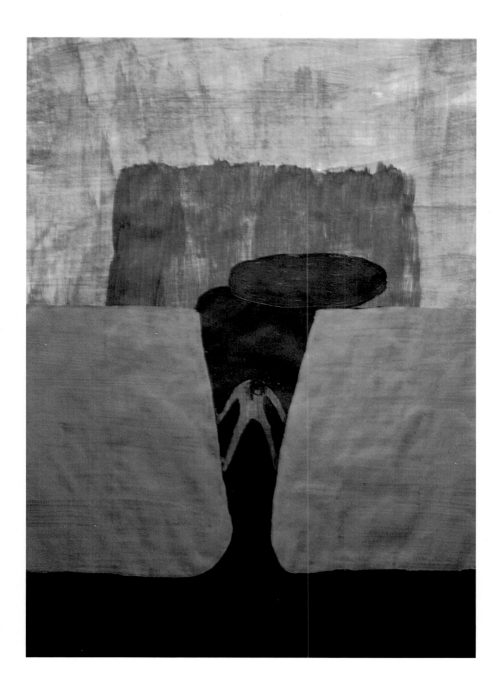

Assault from the Deep

It's come again,
my Leviathan,
relentless and powerful as
before,
dragging me back down
from safety,
back into the undertow.

I thought that I
had passed
from the storm
into the calm,
and that I
could safely walk
into the future
without you
the Leviathan of grief
catching me
unawares,
but I was
wrong,
for today
you came again
gripping me by the throat
and shaking me,
like a dog
with a hare.

Sometimes it seems
more like the flood of
a burst main
pushing its way up
from under the
drain cover
of my life.

But mostly
I just can't put words to it,
only the desolating
sense of loss
that simply becomes
me.

The Wall of Steel

I'm up against a wall,
a wall of hard grey steel,
stretching
in all directions
as far as I can sense
or feel.

It's the cold hard future
through which
no gentle touch
or beckoning voice,
no sound of laughter
or voice of welcome
can penetrate.

I have turned from the past
with its richness
of memories
to the bleakness of the present
where my love is not found,
and I move forward,
and slam into
the unloving
grey wall of steel.

SIX

THE THINGS HE TOUCHED

(Shedding his possessions)

His Ties Still Lie

His ties still lie upon the rack
gently promising
'He might come back,
he just might come back.'

They speak so much of him,
that array of ties,
in bright hues
and bright designs
chosen by him
to speak to others
of his inner self.

Sober they were
when he was young,
with tiny emblems
bright upon
their somberness,
harbingers of future
brightness
and inner light.

In later years
bright tree frogs
cavorted in
obvious joy
before him,
signifying
the flowing laughter
of his spirit
rising to the surface
of his being.

We buried him
wearing the
Bayeux tapestry
in bright richness
so symptomatic
of what this man was,
who loved
this gift of
his daughter.

What am I saying?
We buried him –
who loved life,
truly loved life,
and those who live in it,
for whom tree-frogs
and history
were alike
a source of inquiry,
and of wonder,
and I –
I still keep
his ties.

His Old Decrepit Jacket

His old decrepit jacket
lies in a corner,
rolled up,
out of sight;
but I know it's there.

It's a wax jacket,
worn and stained
from years of use,
protecting him
whom I loved
from the cold
and rain.

It's pockets are torn,
with bits in the seams
that his fingers felt,
their surfaces marked
by his touching.

Some would say
it's old and disgusting
but to me
it's memories encapsulated
and a link with my love.

Twice I have taken it
out from its place,
meaning to throw
it away.

But no, it smells of him,
and speaks to me
of him whom I have lost,
and I put it back.

I've Thrown it Away

I've done it,
I've thrown it away,
that old wax jacket of his
which I loved so much
and which
reminded me of him.

I looked at it
and it was old
and very smelly:
the pockets torn
and folded inside themselves
and the material
tramp-worn in its grim.

That's what it was in itself
or to other people,
but to me,
it was his old wax jacket:
the garment which
had protected him
from bitter winds at Cley
as he watched, delighted,
the bearded tits
and snow buntings.

The coat he had worn,
(when factory fresh)
to walk to church
or go to meetings,
but, as it matured and ripened,
reserved for
more protective duties
in more mundane places:
the collecting of willow twigs
from the
over-wintered lawn,
and his Sunday stroll.

How I miss that jacket
now that I have done
the deed,
but how agonisingly
I miss the person
it represented
who cannot return to me.

Taking it Out Again

I threw his shirt
into the bin,
I did not like it,
but it reminded me of him.
He always started
mowing in it
and, warming up,
removed it
to hang upon the branch
of a convenient tree.

Today,
taking deep breath, I
pushed it down
deep into the rubbish sack
trying not to let
my daughter
see what I did,
nor to think
what it was that I was doing.

Then, after she had gone,
when tidying,
I found it,
tucked away,
in her bottom drawer,
so I buried my face in it
to see if it still
smelled of him.

£5 a Yard

As I'm moving
and I'm down-sizing
I'm selling our memories
books we have bought
through the years
of our marriage,
now boxed up,
taped up,
in incongruous mixes,
to be sold
for five pounds a yard.

As long as I don't think
beyond the stacking
and the packing,
as long as I don't let my mind
dwell
on what these books meant
in our lives,
then all is well.

But then a signature
or words on the fly-leaf
bring back surges of feelings
and I wonder what I am doing
in selling your books
which you loved
so much.

You don't need them now
and you never will again,
but I still feel that
I am letting you down
by selling them,
for you might, just might
need them again.

What value do even
such special things as books
truly have
without you
to share them with?

I Moved His Chair

I moved his chair today.
I moved it
from its place
where he sat
long legs extended
ankles crossed
so familiar,
so familiar,
to me.

I did it,
I moved his chair today
I moved it
from its place
so that I
no longer keep seeing
him sitting there
so familiar
so familiar
to me.

He isn't there,
he isn't really there
and it hurts
to see him
in the eye of my mind
yet not have him there
so familiar
so familiar
to me

Acceptance and His Ties

I know it is a fact
he is dead
and I am not.

I know it is a fact
that I am living
and yet he is dead.

I know it is a fact
that joy is possible
even
after
he has died.

I know it is a fact
I do not need him living
in order
to live myself.

Yet
I also know
it is a fact
that I,
still yearning for his presence,
keep the
iridescence of his ties.

SEVEN

UNDER THE GROUND

(His grave and stone)

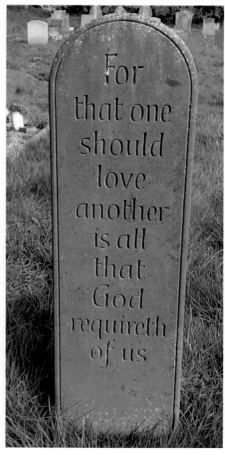

Pink Cherry Blossom

Is my beloved the substance
whereof the
pink cherry blossom
is made?

Together we drove
under an arch
of pink cherry blossom
into our first home
but now he lies
deep in the earth
beneath the tree
which offers cherry blossom
- pink cherry blossom -
to the world.

Pink
the little girls' colour
loved by his daughter
when she was
tiny and ethereal
still loved by her now
in her femininity.

Also beloved of
his mother
as she lies between pink
sheets
in a pink nightie
imagining that it suits her
because
a man once told her
pink suited her
so very many years ago.

Pink cherry blossom
once the symbol of hope
in our marriage
but now greedily
drawing
on the life
that once was his.

Setting His Name in Stone

In the graveyard in the grass
is set a wooden cross
It marks the place where my love lies
a symbol of my a loss.

His name is written on the bar
in lettering of gold
but with the passing of a year
it's fading, dull and old.

It's time for me to think about
a stone to place there now
to tell the ones who yet still live
of him who lies below.

I do not have the words to write
what I would wish to say
of the essence and the life of him
whom death has snatched away.

To see his name written in stone
fills my heart with dread
for this alone will make it clear
that my dear love is dead.

How Can I Express

How can I express to the world
who and what you were
and
what you meant to me?

The plans for the lettering
on your gravestone
came today
and I looked at it
and at your name
and what I had said
and the dates
and, oh my love,
how final,
how overwhelmingly final
it all felt.

I hope I have done you justice
in the eyes of Man
if not in the eyes of God
I hope they will know
that you were extra special
as you lie among those
who were so special too.

What does it mean to write
upon your stone
for lichen, wind and rain to
obscure
that you were a
gentle, humorous
and
intelligent man?

The memories of you
in men's minds
will be limited to your words
in books and papers
and the annals of universities
they will not know of you
what I know of you
all that will have gone.

I don't want gravestones
and beautiful words
I want you, my love,
I want the 'you'
that I have known
and loved,
the one encompassed
in my memories
the 'you' who now belongs
to Someone else
and not to me.

His Stone

His stone stands.
It stands in the churchyard
amongst
the remembrances
of centuries.

His stone is new
and yet is not new;
its colour blends
with the old,
and its meaning
is shared
by them.

It is a thing of beauty
and I am glad
that my beloved's
resting place
is marked
by a
beautiful
stone.

His stone stands
in my mind
as a sign
of completion;
a marker
on the journey
of my life,
one stage over
and another
about to begin.

I will carry
in my mind
the image of that stone
as I carry
within me
the kernel,
the treasure,
of what it meant
to have been
the wife of David
the love of his life
as he was
the love of mine.

I know that
tendrils of mourning
will still come
to catch me unawares,
and fill me with weeping
or flood my eyes
with tears,
but I also know that it is time
to be moving on,
and for that
his stone stands
as a marker
on the way.

I Haven't been to his Grave

I haven't been to his grave
for days and days.
When first he died
it drew me irresistibly
again and again,
my mind torn between
the need to be near
and the fruitlessness
of staying there,
filled with rebellion
that I should be there at all.

The following months
when I knew
that what lay beneath
was no longer him
and that what was there
was not
to be contemplated,
I still clung on
to the fact
that all that remains of him
was there.

Now? Now it's different,
I can go and stand
beside the grassy mound
when I need to,
and not be wracked
by weeping,
or torn apart by the fact
that he lies there.

He has taken his turn
upon the earth,
and it has become
a better place because he lived,
and what more
can be asked of a man
than that?

Now he takes his turn
to lie within the earth,
coffin-cradled
in the clay and loam,
and I can feel
a gentle 'rightness'
about it all,
well, today, now,
for this minute,
I can.

EIGHT

TRYING TO MAKE SENSE
OF 'NOW'

Is this the Wreck?

I this the wreck
of my old life
which
surrounds me
or
the building blocks
of
a new one?

Is it Only in the Remembering

Is it only in the remembering
that you exist,

inhabiting my mind

and the thoughts of those you loved?

Does this mean
that you are only truly dead
when we, too,
have died?

Am I Still Married?

Am I still married
now that he is dead?

According to the law
and
to the scriptures
I am 'free'
(what irony)
to marry again,
so I cannot
be married
to David
anymore.

On forms
I have to put
'single'
not 'married'
just
'single'.

But
inside
I am still
'David's wife'
I am still
married to him
and
I always will be.

In the Powerlessness of Loss

When you died
I became powerless,
or rather,
in your dying,
I have come to know
where I truly stand.

I fight to regain
the control
I once felt I had
over my life
and my future
knowing that
only in your living again
could I feel secure.

And yet...
I am coming to know
that to stand in the space
where others
(dispossessed)
also stand,
is to be where
Jesus stood
before Pilate,
and that I should not seek
to grasp again
the illusion of power
that I once held.

Once I was a 'Me'

Once I was a 'Me'
a word spoken by God,
complete and whole,
one being.

Then I met my love,
and in love's meeting,
became one flesh
a new being.

All through the years
we grew together
interwoven
tightly bound.

Until all our thoughts
our minds and living
were united
in our 'Us'.

Then death did us part
and in that parting
tore our union
into two.

As the months go by
I ask the question
can I be 'me'
once again?

What is left of me
that can exist alone
when half of me
isn't here?

Somewhere inside me
there must still be
the essential being
which makes me,
me?

The Crying Place

There's a place in the garden
where two old hedges meet,
Two slender trunks
lean for support
with their barks scarred
from ponies chewing:
it's the place we go to cry.

The ground is brown with
last year's leaves
trodden and brushed
into the soil.
Decaying branches
twigs and leaves
are piled up there,
the secret hiding place
of living things.

That place is a refuge for us,
in our grief,
a place where we can go
and stand
faces averted from the world
unmolested and alone
and weep to feel
the loss and pain inside.

The day that David died
it became a special place,
the scarred and broken branches
from the slashing, ripping,
hedge cutter
echoing our brokenness
and our despair.

Since then that place
has seen and received our tears
as we have poured out to God,
and to the air,
our loss and grief and fears
to be carried away on the wind.

The scars on those trees
are healing,
the bark is growing round them,
will we one day be mended too?
The trunks will not be
as they were,
they'll have a different form
reflecting the injury;
and the healing too,
will it be the same for us?

Alone in the House

Sometimes there is freedom
in being alone;
being alone in the house.

Before you died
I used to cherish
time alone,
knowing that it would end
in the greeting
of your returning
and the loving embrace.

Even now,
in the daytime,
I can sometimes feel
that freedom,
not tied by other's needs
even the needs of those I love.

But then
there's the emptiness
of aloneness,
the profound silence
of the night
with the only the chorus
of my racing blood
in my ears,
and no human sound
whatsoever.

Then the sound
of voices on the radio
and television's many faces
become my company,
faint substitutes for yours
and the medicine
of distraction.

I have to learn
that I am not alone;
to ask God to fill for me
the gap you left behind,
and
like Elijah,
I have to hear His voice
in the still calm point
of the storm
of your loss.

It's a Beautiful Thing

In the beginning
of this
millennium
in the howling grey
(deserted)
emptiness
of your going
hearing only the
insistent
refrain
'David is dead'
'David is dead'
I was made a
priest.

"It is a beautiful
thing
you do today"
the preacher said.

What did he mean?
What has it all
been for?
Even now
(some years on)
I struggle with your
going
(and my
loss).
I cannot
make sense
of my life
or my priesting,
and in the dark
of the night

wish that I were dead
and with you
once again.

I am empty, my love.
I have nothing left
to give.
I need you here
in the bed
to hold me,
in the house
to share with me
in my life
to be with me.
Memories
are not enough.

"It's a beautiful thing
you do today."
Why?

Lord,
help me
to understand.

There is no Space for Grieving

There is no space
for grieving
as the years go by,
and
expectations
change.

'Her husband died
some years ago,
but she has
picked up the pieces
and
moved on.'

Well, I have
moved on,
and thrown away
the pieces,
or had them
taken away.

And now,
when I weep
I do so
in secret
for who
could understand
that the knife
still cuts as sharp
even though
it is not new?

Pressing Escape

I have a purple tee-shirt
with writing on the front,
bought on holiday
when we two were one.
It simply says:-
'I keep hitting the escape key
but I am still here.'

For two and a half years
I have longed to press
the escape key
and be gone,
and the edges of the fabric
of the shirt
have become worn and frayed
with use.

But today
I saw it in the cupboard
and I rejected it,
because today, and now,
I want to live.

Maybe one day
I will cut it up
and make it
into a picture,
a contract with God;
who alone should press
the 'escape' key.

but not yet…

I Saw and Smelled and Felt You

I saw and smelled and felt you
as you leaned towards me
for a kiss;
but then I awoke
back into the knowledge
that you no longer live
and sadness
and yearning poured into me
again.

It is strange
that when you lived
I never dreamt of you
but now you are dead,
and have been dead
for several years
you are so often there
alive and busy
in my dreams.

Can I Learn...

Can I learn
to live without you?
Without your love?
Do I have to accept that
I will not have
your loving again?
Is there a place, a space,
where living
without your love
is possible?

It seems that I
am rejecting you
when I say such things,
admitting that I can live
without you,
and have transient joy and peace
in that living,
but you know my love,
there are times now
when I just get on with life,
accepting your absence
as permanent,
and, almost,
'just the way things are.'

But then, daily it seems,
there is within me
rebellion,
for I do not want to have to learn
to live without your love;
to be what I did not choose to be
a David-less widow.
I do not want to say
that I can do without you;
and yet
I must learn to live that way,
and to live the life
that I yet have
as a gift.

Yesterday, I Gave Him Back

Yesterday I gave him back,
the one I loved so well,
who alone was one with me
body, mind and spirit
intertwining.
But I gave him back
– back to the one
who lent him to me,
he was not really mine
just borrowed.

Meeting, we had loved,
and in the years of loving,
grown to be
a blend of him and me:
our marriage.

Blending, we had cradled
new loves living
growing into person hood
– the fruits of our loving
in God's designs.

Working and playing,
we had grown to understand
our oneness,
and did not comprehend
that we were two.

But then the very thing
which made us two
became of itself
our nemesis
and our undoing.

But he, the one I loved,
was torn from me,
and in his dying
he left me clinging
to hopeless hopes.

Four seasons have been
and in their passing
I have hoped for his
returning
against all hope.

Put not your trust in princes
or in loving men,
for they will surely die
their spirits turning to the Lord
and bodies to earth again.

So yesterday I gave him back
to the One who loves him most,
and I saw him in His arms,
loved in the heavens
as here on earth
and I wept.

NINE

OUT OF THE VALLEY...

My Mind is Surging

My mind is surging
between
last year's grief
and next year's hope.

Am I married?
or am I not?
Am I a single women
free to make my own decisions
without reference
to David's mind?
Or will I for ever be
held by the chord's of love
into knowing his mind
in my thinking?

I think I know
that I am becoming
my own person
as I drift further
from the ship
of David's holding
and his loving;
I can still see the
vessel of our marriage
which held us
but I know
the lifeboat which now holds
me
is going
to a different
destination.

I know too
that, much of the time,
I am turning to face
the way the boat
is going,
that I do not spend
so much time
looking back,
desperately rowing
against the tide.

I am glad
the boat I'm in
was launched from
that particular ship,
for deep inside of me
I know of the cargo
of loving
that was held there
and how it changed me,
and that,
in some way,
I carry some of it
to the place
where I am going
on my own.

The Widow's Wail

Have you heard?
have you heard
the cry in the heart, or upon the
lips,
of the woman
when the cloak of widowhood
descends upon her?

Have you felt it in you,
emerging from your throat,
unbidden,
unexpected,
howling to the world
the pain,
the awful pain,
in your heart?

Do you know how
it changes
as days, weeks,
or even months go by,
and your loss
becomes embedded
in your soul,
and the wail becomes
the howl of despair
in the loss of hope?

Have you heard its note
change within you:
softer,
and gentler,
as you accept
the place where you are,
and weep for times
gone by?

And do you know
do you know
that God hears your cry,
do you know
how great is his love
for widows,
and that he's there
in your suffering?

I have known
these things,
so I carry within me
that first unbelieving scream
– unuttered –
tearing my mind apart.
I also hold within me
the gentler cry,
and the knowledge
of God's loving heart.

A Different Spring

The snowdrops are opening
in innocent perfection,
complementing
winter aconites
under the hazel trees.

Can you see them my love?
Can you see them?
They are early this year
bringing promise of Spring.

And this year, my love,
as I hear the songs of the birds
change their tunes
to songs of love,
my heart has lifted,
and hope has filled me,
for a brief moment,
I have been happy,
truly happy.

Climbing the Mountain

A welsh farm
amongst the gentle
aged mountains
slow rolling
their way
over the face
of the earth.

Friend by friend
ascending the mountain-track,
arduous, yet mind-filling,
contrast of struggling body
and familiar
much-loved
sheep-cropped grass
dark droppings
and coal-black slugs,
and over all,
the sound of sheep
and rejoicing larks.

Stopping to breath
and absorb the view
of farm and living
far below.

Coming to the crown
with wind-washed grasses
and distance, such distance,
all around.

Companionable looking,
sharing, talking,
and the domestic glory
of the Mid-Wales countryside
spread out below
for our eyes.

Then, familiar also,
the knowledge,
that were I to spread my wings,
I could fly through
that clear space
like an eagle.

No longer the desire
to plunge down to oblivion,
instead life calls,
and the joy of rushing air
and shared identity
with the song of the lark.

Deep Water

Last year I sat
in the depths of despair
watching
the deep black flowing
of the river,
knowing
that I wanted to be
enfolded,
absorbed,
into it depths.

The river was
flowing
powerfully
relentlessly
onwards
holding within it
the possibility
of drowning
and leaving;
breathing its
deep
life-extinguishing
life-restoring
waters.

This year I felt the Lord say
'Come aside with me,
come play on the river
with your boat.'

So I went there again
and saw how
beautiful
is the river,
how it flowed beneath me
moving the leaves
of the water plants,
the flowers
of the lilies
were gently rocked
on its surface.

The swallows and the bats
swooped and swerved
over its generous surface
which gives them life.

Trailing branches
of the trees
tenderly touch the water
in looping ripples,
and,
dodging one of these,
I fell in,
up to my neck
in the flowing river!

And in my splashing
deep under water,
and rising again to
catch the boat
and its oars,
struggling to land,
jellyfish-like,
in its coracle safety,
I laughed at myself,
at what I had done,
what I had achieved,
and God showed me
how far I have come.

Soft Joy in the Hills

There in Wales
it was a soft day
a soft day of mists
and rain
and Spring sunshine.
The misty colour of bluebells
amongst the young oaks
gentle hope
of life to come.

There on the paths
my heart lifted
my spirit received the balm
which comes
from His creation
amongst the
undulating hills
and forests
where I feel at home
my whole body relaxed
into relief,
and my spirit
into soft joy.

There in the hills
I did not miss you
so acutely
but remembered you
with love and gratitude
for having walked with me
through this transient life
for just a little while,
or so it seems to me.

There, in the hills,
and on those paths of Spring,
I knew and felt
a future,
a possible future,
in which you
are just a memory
treasured in my past,
no longer holding me
back.

I Awoke with a Smile

I awoke with a smile this morning
a brief spell of happiness
before the knowledge
of his loss
came flooding back again.

In my dream it had been
Christmas day
and we were walking
playing together,
carrying gifts
for his parents.

He turned to me and laughed
and smiled
at something he saw there.
In deep joy we went on,
and arriving,
caused his parents to
roll around the floor
in laughter.

In laughter too I looked
at my face
in the mirror
only to see that
whilst we had played
my love had stuck a cherry
on my nose,
which, squinting, I could see
but had not seen.

For the joy of that dream,
for being with him again
I thank you Lord.

Home

Home is beginning to feel
like 'home' again,
friendly, welcoming,
and enfolding.
It does not shout so much
of David's death,
but more of the living
who celebrated
Christmas,
lived and grew,
and played here,
of jokes shared,
and tumbling laughter.

When I open the door
the house no longer says to me
'I am empty',
but 'Come in my friend,
you are welcome here.'

What has made the change?
just as I am coming
to the time
when I must put into motion
the selling of
this house, this home,
and leave it?

Maybe it's just not thinking,
not thinking about him,
nor looking at his picture,
not letting thoughts of him
creep into the cracks of
my mind.

But maybe it's that I am
becoming used to living here
without him,
unbelievable
as that may seem.

TEN

MOVING ON...

Tonight and Tomorrow I Dance

Tonight I dance with you my love
and hold the air where once you were.
I feel again your hand upon my shoulder
and your arm about my waist,
with the joy and love
which was in your dancing.

The waltzes from Vienna
playing the old year to its end
and the new year from
its beginning
and you dancing again with me
in my remembering.

Thank you for dancing with me
stumble footed as I was,
thank you for leaving me
the memory to dance with now
to feel again the love you gave to me
and to treasure it.

I thought you would not enter
into this new year with me,
but you are here
in the space between
my dancing arms
in our loving
and in
my remembering.

Footnote
*(Every New Year's Eve, just before the turning of the year, the BBC
used to play waltzes from Vienna, and David and I would dance
together, so that we entered the new year in each other's arms.)*

I Have Taken Down

I have taken down
the hanging branches
which draped the picture
frames,
the holly and the ivy
which wound their way along
the beams,
and across the fireplace,
and the bright sparkling
tinsel bits
which hid among them.

I have folded up the
fairy lights
which also wended their way
along the beam
and shone in the dark fireplace
like glorious stars.

I have stripped the Christmas-
tree of its glory,
and put it heavily away,
the baubles and icicles
now trapped in boxes.

The stars and the angels,
which moved gently
in response
to our passing
along the corridor,
now lie hidden, motionless
in old biscuit tins.

The paper holly leaves
with scarlet berries
once made by childish hands
to brighten up the walls
of the hall
and greet the visitor
with the message
'Christmas is coming!'
are carefully laid away.

The bright tinsel wreathes
twisted among green leaves
that embellished the
grandfather clock,
and the bookcases,
are all stowed away
for the last time.

And as I pack up
these precious things
which speak to me of
so many years of happiness,
of childish voices, laughter,
of tearing paper,
shared friendship, and dinners
– delicious, anticipated,
hunger-enhanced dinners –
I gave thanks.

For I do not know where,
– or even if –
those boxes will be opened
again,
but I do know it won't be here
and it won't be the same.

Next year I will celebrate
in a different time,
and a different place.
These memories
that I have packed away
will always be softly there
in my mind for me to treasure.

Tomorrow is Epiphany,
and I will move forward
into the new life
that is the gift from God to me,
I will place my hand in His
and let Him lead me
into the darkness
where He himself is the light.

A Letter of Condolence

It had been hidden there
through the seasons from his dying,
unopened and unread,
waiting to jettison me again
into the awful pain
of that time.

But in it, among the kindly words
the expressions of concern
and promises to uphold
was a verse, a Bible verse
which leapt out at me.

"The Lord is close to the
broken-hearted
and saves those
who are crushed in spirit."
A word of comfort to me
from my God.

Grand Finale for a House

A garden full of celebration
for a house
which has sheltered us
for more than
a quarter of a century.

This house has held us
whilst we loved
and have been loved.
It has received the laughter
– and the crying –
of babies, children
and of me.

It has been filled with
joyous sunshine,
sheltered us from the rain,
and been our window
to the glories of the garden
and the wonders
of the world outside.

And the garden has been full
of running legs
and young voices
embracing the future
and the imaginary
whilst combining the two.

It is also the place
where the Lord himself
bent down
to touch my heart
revealing himself
in tender joy.

Now it's time to say
'Thank you' and to celebrate
with flags and friends
and
sky-filling fireworks
the gift we have had
in living here
and then
to depart.

In our leaving
is also the praying
that those who come after
will be blessed
in the knowledge
of the Lord,
and
abundant laughter,
as we have been.

Twenty-Five Years

The furniture is piled
in heaps,
the books are in boxes,
and the walls are bare,
and I look about me
and remember.

Twenty five years ago
the furniture
was piled in heaps
waiting to be unpacked,
and the background
to my circling exhaustion
was running feet
and childish laughter,
sharing the chaos
with you,
the one I depended on.

Do you remember my love,
(house...
do you remember too?)
how those tiny feet thundered
along the corridor
and jumped and thumped
over the step,
only to turn and run and jump
again?

We grew this house around us
as a tortoise grows its shell,
every bit of it
speaks of our planning
and our dreams,
even the dreams
as yet unrealised
and now,
never to be so.

This house was our shared
creation,
unlike any other house,
old and unique,
and ours,
and full of sunshine.

But now
I have to let you both go,
the one so dearly beloved
the other a framing cradle,
an old master,
a backdrop,
for our loving.

Unpacking the Comfort Blanket

They have lain
in dark and musty boxes
since we
incarcerated them
so many months ago
in another time
and
another part
of my life.

Then I was being
torn apart
in the losing
and
the letting go.

Each book
held its own
measure of pain
for me.

But now I greet
old friends
and place them
comfortably
around me
in the building up
of the new
and,
once again,
they form the
comfort blanket
around me.

Different Paths

Four years ago
today
(almost to the hour)
you died.
I did not understand
that we had come
to a
parting
of the ways.

I thought
you had gone
and that
I
had been left
behind.

Looking back,
I can now see
that
not only
had you gone
(and 'going'
must have gone
somewhere)
but I also
have been travelling
a divergent path.

When our children
were little
we took them
and left them
at the school gate
until, after
the working day,
we returned,
to be re-united
with them
once more.

And so,
today,
I say to you,
my love,
that I am leaving you
(as it were)
at the gates of heaven
and I am going
on my own path,
(as myself)
wherever God may lead me
until such time
as I, also,
reach those gates.

I do not know
in what way
re-uniting
occurs
in the intention
of God,
but I trust
that it will be
good.

Gentle Company

Yesterday I visited
people you do not know
and never met.
I visited them
and was enfolded
and received
into the warm peace
of their home,
and knew again something
I had not known
since you died.

In our sitting,
in our talking,
and in our silences
there was no tension
only
an acceptance of being
and of God's presence
with us.

And you know, my love,
that their love for each other
was hospitable
for me,
and when I came away
I knew my loss
in the leaving,
my loss of what we had had
you and I,
our fully accepting
companionship,
and I yearned for it
as I wept.

But I also knew
that there was a place
where it all
still exists.

I Can Imagine *(On my Son's Wedding Day)*

The day before their wedding
anticipation
of good things to come,
joyful,
scurrying, preparations
and moments
of calm –
I can imagine you there
happy and full of
fatherly
contentment
with what your son
is about to do.

I can imagine the sound
of your voice
as you sit with
your sister,
and your aunt,
and your nephew,
deeply interested
in what they say.

I can imagine you
greeting
each of your sons
as they arrive,
to help carry,
and arrange,
and get things done,
you would have put your arms
right around them
as they put theirs
around you.

I can imagine you there
in the morning
reading your paper
over the hotel breakfast,
and
just chatting
with the family.

I can imagine your pleasure
as your daughter arrives
and hear the lilt of joy
in your voice
as you see her
and envelop her
in your cavernous hug.

I can see your eyes
fill with tears
as your son stands
so proudly beside his bride
hands linked behind his back,
and then again
as they say their vows,
reflecting the tears
which rim
the bride's.

As they sign the register
you would have taken
the camera
and captured their delight
in each other and that moment.

Then, as they processed
out of the church
you would have walked
with her mother,
as I walked with her father,
so pleased to be doing so.

I can imagine
how proud
you would have been,
and moved too,
by the speeches
your sons made,
and I suspect that
they would have filled you
with both tears and laughter.

And I can imagine
how you would
have talked
and played
with your new grandchildren,
and they would have been
totally
amused.

But most of all,
I can imagine you
amongst the guests
at the celebration,
and I know you would
have laughed and smiled
and shared yourself,
amongst young and old,
family and friends,
and those whom you had
never met before,
and you would have danced -
oh, how you would have
danced!

It was a good day
a special joy-filled day
a day for proud father-ship
and you would have loved it,
so I am glad
that I can imagine
you there amongst us,
glad that
what I can imagine
is true to you,
so that
your absence
adds not only
to my sorrow,
but also,
abundantly
to my great joy.

Colour Me Black Today

Colour me black today,
let the material
that encloses my body
hold in itself
the warp and weft
of my being.

'Why don't you wear
something
just a bit more
colourful?'
they say,
'it might make you
feel a little better'.

Obediently,
I encase myself
in brighter cloth
but it isn't me;
it isn't me at all,
and I fling it aside
in despair.

I have a need
for my outer covering,
to share the darkness
which has invaded me,
and I find inside
an aversion
to being visible
in the remaining shadows
of our life.

Colour Me Rose and Gold

Colour me rose and gold,
array me in
kingfisher blue
or
gladioli scarlet
or
a lavender hue.

Cast a light through a prism
and let me dress
in spectrum colours!

Let the joy in living
and loving
which now
inhabits
me
outhabit
me too.

For on Saturday,
on SATURDAY!
we celebrated
three new years
of marriage,
and life
is worth
the living
again.

ELEVEN

GIVING THANKS ...
FOR THE TREASURES
OF DARKNESS.

The Amphitheatre of God.

*Darkness is
the amphitheatre of God
giving space
for him
to act.*

It's in the Darkest Places

It's in the darkest places
that I've found You Lord.

These long months
since my beloved died,
have seen me
wracked
and hurled
between the rocks
of outrageous pain.

And yet, if you were to ask me,
I would live them again
in order to learn
what I have learned
of You.

For in the darkest places
I found you Lord,
I have known you in ways
not possible before,
and I immerse
myself in You.

The Basket of Light

I sense a basket of light
woven around me
in this darkness deeper than night
keeping me from descending
into the pit.

They say that man is made
in the image of God
and that the light that does not fade
is the Spirit
indwelling.

A soft and gentle glowing
is the light from each heart
that keeps me from growing
self-centred and
apart.

Long ago, a woman made
a basket of rushes
and in it gently laid her son
to float upon
the Nile

And so, like a basket of light
woven around me
in this darkness deeper than night
is the God-side of people
and I give thanks.

Garments of Praise

We sing a song, Lord,
a song of Isaiah,
a song you once sung
to your people,
of how you would give them
a crown of beauty
instead of ashes,
oil of gladness
instead of mourning,
and a garment of praise
instead of despair.

You were singing a love song
to your people who mourned,
and I,
in my mourning,
ask you to sing that song to me,
and to give me those things
which will fill my heart
with songs of praises for you.

The death of beautiful things is all around us, and so is the birth of beautiful things

The Death of Beautiful Things

The death of beautiful things
is all around.
The glory of the feathers
on the neck of a pheasant
lie jewel-scattered
on the trampled grass,
a sacrament
of its death.

Snow-like on the lawn
also lie the petals
of the once so fragrant
spring-innocent
apple blossom.

Welling up in the sky
is the heart-swelling
glory
of the sunset,
transient
and gone
into the dull darkness
of the night.

Yes, all around me,
is the death of beautiful things,
extending from
earth-lip to earth-lip
around the globe,
baby, flower
and dream of God
all gone together.

But, slow, over the dawn
horizon
comes the renewed glory
and
deep within the buds,
inside living bodies
new sources of beauty
have their conception
and their growing.

And as I watch my sons
and daughter
I see the birth
of the ideas sown by their father
the gift of living
in friendship and laughter
and
the loving
way of being,
the reverse
rainbowed shadow
of his dying.

Come Dance With Me

At prayer
in the silence of the evening
in the convent chapel
I felt the Lord say
Do you want to dance?
for I would like to dance with you
in my creation ..
and I 'saw' Him take me by the hand
and dance with me
among the flowers
of the upland meadows.

He took delight in me
and, in my mind's eye,
I danced with Him and laughed with Him
as a child
released from its chores
will do.

Then again,
another time.
being with Him
amongst His people
and answering again His call
'Come dance with Me'
I took courage
and went in
among the dancing people
and shared with them
His love
in the dancing
and the meeting
and holding of gaze
and knowing that
heaven and earth
were meeting
in His dance.

It Seems That Joy

It seems that joy
– like a magnet –
draws to itself
despair;
and that love
– evolving –
draws to itself
pain.

For the greatest evil
and the greatest pain
are found beside
manifest good
and revelation
of joy.

And where God is
– and where God was –
evil deeds abound
man abuses Man
and heaven is haunted
by hell.

Or could it be
that despair
– like a magnet –
draws to itself Joy,
and evil attracts mercy
in the attention span
of God;
and hell is haunted
by heaven?

The Baby

The baby lies
enfolded in the womb,
warm and safe
no knowledge yet of birth.

The sounds he hears
conception taught him first
his fingers touch
only soft and gentle curves.

His time has come
the crushing and the pain,
love is pushing
him out into the world.

What has he done
to deserve this birthing
this offering
of a human life to live?

The people gather
rejoicing at this birth
united in thanks
for a safe arrival.

The baby is
embarking on its journey
A life is lived
familiar in its days.

*   *   *

But now,
his end has come
seemingly untimely,
death is pushing
him out of this world.
What has he done
to deserve this dying
the ending of
many years of living?

Or is this too
renewal and birthing
the proper end
and a new beginning?

And do the heavens
with singing and dancing
unite in thanks
and praise for his soul?

And does our God
with tenderness and joy
reach out to him
and welcome him home?

TWELVE

EPILOGUE

If I Had the Courage

If I had the courage
I would howl your name to the heavens
till it echoed through the hollows of the hills,
I would send it roaring down the valleys in rivers
then ricocheting through the roads of the towns.

I would send it sashaying along the aisles
in the supermarket
and rending the air in the church
I would hurl it round the tops of the chimneys
and sliding along the slates of the roofs.

As a sibilant whisper through the reeds
I would send it
and as a thundering roar through the waves
I would volley it down through volcanoes
to rattle the core of the earth
I would stun the sun into silence
and place it in the mouth of the moon.
I would wrap it in a sonnet of singing
and post it off to the stars...

If I had the courage.

ACKNOWLEDGEMENTS

I would like to thank all those who pushed me into publishing these poems, including Natalie Watson (then at MPH) Esther Shreeve, (and the most persistent of all) Helen Ward. A number of people have helped me sort them and decide which of the 500 plus poems should go in, and which be left out, and I would really like to thank Kate Litchfield, Wendy Shaw, Helen Ward and Anna Green for being so helpful over this. I am immensely grateful to you all, and to Jennifer Kharibian, who has helped me edit and sort them a final time. All mistakes and blunders are entirely mine.

I also a debt of gratitude to Chris Powell and Pete Goddard at Verité, who have encouraged me to publish, and not complained about my rather chaotic way of approaching the whole venture.

Some of my poems have been published in *The Gingerbread House* by Esther Shreeve.